Taste and See Faith:
Recipes for the Soul

By Marie Wilson

Published by
Bezalel Books
Waterford, MI

Visit our website for inspirational Christian fiction and non-fiction books.
www.BezalelBooks.com

Printed in the United States of America

ISBN 978-0-9794976-5-0
Library of Congress Control Number 2007931717

"KNOW THAT THE LORD WORKS WONDERS FOR THE FAITHFUL"

The title of this page comes from Psalm 4:4 - Trust in God. As a Christian and author, I have been searching my mind and soul for a new and different angle to spread the Good News about Jesus. My prayers were answered when the idea for a Christian recipe book with faith information came to me. Taste and See Faith is the result of Trusting in God.

I have learned that it takes more than just trusting in God to complete his works. It takes patience, understanding, and support from family and friends. And so, I would like to thank my husband Dave; daughters Angie, Becky, and Megan; and my mother Dolores for supporting me so I may do God's work in writing this wonderful Christian Recipe Book. I would also like to thank everyone who provided "yummy" recipes for this book.

May God bless you all!

TELL GOD'S GLORY AMONG THE NATIONS; AMONG ALL PEOPLES, GOD'S MARVELOUS DEEDS. PSALM 96:3

Advent

O Come, O Come Emmanuel

O Come, O Come Emmanuel is a clear message that we prepared ourselves, our homes and churches to receive the Messiah into our lives. We started our preparation and expectation of Christ four Sundays before the Christmas Season the second greatest season of our church year; Easter being the first greatest season.

Advent should be somewhat low-keyed and penitential in tone from the start and then build up to a joyous celebration on Christmas Day. The colors of purple and rose are used to indicate passion and subdued joy. There are various symbols used to help prepare ourselves for Christ's coming.

The Advent wreath with three purple candles and one rose color candle decorated with boughs of holly symbolizes anticipation of Christ's coming. For the first two Sundays, two purple candles are lit which focus on Jesus' final coming as Lord and judge. On the third Sunday, two purple and the rose candles are lit. The joy of Christ's coming is building more within us. On the last Sunday of Advent all four candles are lit to anticipate his coming in history (Christ-mas). This is a time of jubilation for Christ is nearly here!

How will you prepare for Christ's coming; perhaps an empty Crèche display in your home? The Crèche is a picturesque nativity scene. Each Sunday an item can be added to the Crèche such as stable animals, straw, and shepherds. On Christmas Day, the Crèche should be complete with Baby Jesus, Mary, Joseph, angels, and the Star of Bethlehem which represents David, house of Jesus' family.

The placement of a single candle in each window of the home is another way to show we are ready to receive Christ and welcome him into our lives. Will you decorate your home with poinsettia plants that signify the Star of Bethlehem? The red poinsettia plants show love of Christ. Legend states that the carnation first appeared at the birth of Christ and has been named the flower of rejoicing. All these symbols point to Christ our Savior, the one who cleanses our souls from sin so we may enter the Kingdom of God.

The Paschal mystery is unfolded during the time of Advent. There is the cycle of feasts surrounding the mystery of the incarnation. They are: Annunciation (Archangel Gabriel announces to Mary she will conceive a child through the Holy Spirit), Christmas, and Epiphany. These feasts are the foot paths to the beginning of our salvation and shows honor to us the first fruits of the Paschal mystery.

We need to pray during Advent as a sign to God we are willing to open our hearts to receive his Son. We need to be more like Mary who accepted God's will. "I am the Lord's servant," said Mary, "may it happen to me as you have said." Luke 1:38. Advent is the dawning of great things to come. It is the beginning of fulfilling the prophecies of the Old Testament.

Advent is a time to reflect, to prepare, to anticipate and rejoice in Christ's birth. The songs we sing in church reflect our preparation. Songs like: O Come, O Come Emmanuel, Proclaim the Joyful Message, and People, Look East sets the mood for the Christmas Season. Open your hearts and minds to receive the blessing God will bestow upon us. Let the Holy Spirit guide you during Advent so you may be ready to receive Christ into you life.

"IN THE DESERT PREPARE THE WAY OF THE LORD! MAKE STRAIGHT IN THE WASTELAND A HIGHWAY FOR OUR GOD!" ISAIAH, 40:3

THANKSGIVING SPICE COOKIE

¾	Cup brown sugar
¾	Cup sugar
1	Cup butter
1	Teaspoon vanilla
1	Teaspoon water
2	Eggs
2	Cups flour
1	Teaspoon salt and 1 teaspoon baking soda
1	Cup Heath toffee bits
1	Cup Cinnamon chips
1	Cup chopped walnuts (optional)

Beat the butter, sugars, water, eggs, and vanilla together. Add baking soda and salt. Slowly mix in flour. Fold in Heath toffee bits, cinnamon chips and nuts. Place batter on a lightly greased 12-inch diameter pizza pan. Pre-heat oven at 350° F. Bake for 35 minutes. There will be a little gooeyness when a toothpick is used to check for doneness.

"TO YOU WE OWE OUR HYMN OF PRAISE, O GOD ON ZION; TO YOU OUR VOWS MUST BE FULFILLED, YOU WHO HEAR OUR PRAYERS." PSALMS 65:2

Calico Bean Dish

2	Pounds of ground beef, cooked and drained
½	Pound bacon, cooked and cut into small pieces
1	Whole onion chopped
¾	Cups brown sugar
2	Tablespoons mustard
2	Tablespoons apple vinegar
1	Tablespoon garlic salt
1	Can lima beans drained – little green ones
1	Can good pork and beans
1	Can dark kidney beans drained

Mix all ingredients and place in a baking dish. Bake for 45 minutes at 350° F. This recipe tastes like a barbeque!

"KNOW THAT THE LORD WORKS WONDERS FOR THE FAITHFUL; THE LORD HEARS WHEN I CALL OUT. PSALMS 4:4

PUMPKIN LOG

3 Eggs; ¾ Cup sugar; 2/3 Cup pumpkin; 1 Teaspoon baking soda
1 Teaspoon cinnamon; ¾ Cup flour

Beat eggs till lemon colored, add sugar slowly, add pumpkin, and dry ingredients, and mix well. Bake in greased jelly roll pan 17 ¼ x 11 ½ x 1-inch (grease pan then put wax paper on top then grease the top of the wax paper). Bake at 350 degrees for 15 minutes. Roll up after it is removed from the oven and let cool 15 to 20 minutes.

Filling:

2 Tblspns margarine; ¾ Teaspoon vanilla;1 Cup confectioners sugar; 1 8 ounce cream cheese, softened.

Mix well. Unwrap roll (make sure to remove the wax paper first) and spread with filling, roll up and wrap up in the same wax paper and then wrap with tin foil, store in refrigerator. This also freezes well.

"BUT STORE UP TREASURES IN HEAVEN, WHERE NEITHER MOTH NOR DECAY DESTROY, NOR THIEVES BREAK IN AND STEAL. FOR WHERE YOUR TREASURE IS, THERE ALSO WILL YOUR HEART BE."
MATTHEW 6:20-21

GOULASH CASSEROLE

1 Pound box of elbow noodles - cook to directions on box
1 Jar of spaghetti sauce (26 ounce)
1 Package of shredded mozzarella cheese (12 ounce)
½ to 1 Pound lean ground beef

Brown the meat and drain the fat. Add the spaghetti sauce and let simmer until heated through. Mix the meat/sauce with the cooked noodles and place in a baking dish 13x9x2 inch. Sprinkle cheese on top. Preheat oven at 350° F and bake uncovered until cheese is thoroughly melted, approximately 30 minutes. Serves about 6.

WHEN ELIZABETH HEARD MARY'S GREETING, THE INFANT LEAPED IN HER WOMB, AND ELIZABETH, FILLED WITH THE HOLY SPIRIT, CRIED OUT IN A LOUD VOICE AND SAID, "MOST BLESSED ARE YOU AMONG WOMEN, AND BLESSED IS THE FRUIT OF YOUR WOMB." LUKE 1:41-42

"WESTERNS" HAMBURG PATTIES

½ Pound ground beef
4 to 5 Eggs
Salt and pepper to taste

Mix all ingredients together. On a hot griddle, spoon 2 spoonfuls of egg/beef mixture to form a 5 inch diameter patty. Turn patty over when the edges look dry, similar to a pancake.

ONE MIGHTIER THAN I IS COMING AFTER ME.
I AM NOT WORTHY TO STOOP AND LOOSEN THE THONGS OF
HIS SANDALS.
I HAVE BAPTIZED YOU WITH WATER;
HE WILL BAPTIZE YOU WITH THE HOLY SPIRIT.
MARK 1:7-8

OPEN OUR HEARTS, PREPARE THE WAY

The dawning of Advent is upon us and the regeneration of spiritual needs is at hand. O Heavenly Father God of great love, we pray for the Holy Spirit to help us prepare for the coming of your son Jesus. We ask for guidance so we may take the right actions, say the right words, and think the right thoughts so the path to our door will be clear and straight. We open our minds and hearts to receive the Holy Spirit and absorb her wisdom; the wisdom that is holy and righteous. Heavenly Father, hear our prayer and know we want to receive the Light of the World into our lives. Amen

Christmas Season

LIGHT OF THE WORLD

A white candle signifying the purity of conception and birth of Christ is lit on Christmas Day the start of the Christmas Season. The Christmas Season lasts until Epiphany Sunday. There are five feasts celebrated during this time. They are: Christmas, Holy Family, Mary, Mother of God, Epiphany, and the Baptism of our Lord.

December 25th was the date chosen as the birth of Christ, the Light of the World. The traditional midnight Mass on Christmas Eve is believed to be the hour that Christ was born. Whether we celebrate Christ's birth at midnight Mass or on Christmas Day, it is important to attend Mass. Mass helps bring fulfillment within us, especially when it is celebrated with family.

The feast of the Holy Family is celebrated the Sunday after Christmas. This feast commemorates Mary and Joseph who did not hesitate to do what God asked of them - to be the mother and father to Jesus. When there was danger, Joseph acted upon God's command to take Mary and Jesus to Egypt. He kept them there until it was safe to return back to Israel.

"Rise, take the child and his mother, flee to Egypt, and stay there until I tell you. Herod is going to search for the child to destroy him." Matthew 2:13

January 1st brings us the feast of Mary, Mother of God. Mary has been noted throughout the years as "Mary, Star of Evangelization" by Pope Paul VI or "The Mother of the Redeemer" by Pope John Paul II. During Mass, Mary is mentioned in the creeds, the Eucharistic Prayer, and to some extent in the penitential rite. Mary holds many titles such as "Our Lady of Guadalupe," or "Our Mother of Perpetual Help." The Rosary is associated with Mary and there are countless songs, praises, and scriptures that honor her.

The Three Wise Men (Magi) arrived 12 days after Christmas which is Epiphany Sunday. Epiphany is celebrated the Sunday after January 1st. "...and on entering the house they saw the child with Mary his mother. They prostrated themselves and did him homage." Mt. 2:11. Epiphany is the manifestation of Jesus as Messiah of Israel, Son of God and Savior of the world. The three wise men were witnesses of the manifestation of Christ.

The Christmas season is rounded out by the baptism of Jesus. This blessed event is celebrated the Sunday after Epiphany. John the Baptist foretells of Jesus' coming, the Messiah, to be baptized with water and filled with the Holy Spirit. The baptism of Jesus with water symbolizes the cleansing of sins and renewal of faith. The Holy Spirit gave knowledge and wisdom to Jesus so he may teach the peoples of Israel about the Kingdom of God.

The Christmas Season does not appear to be long, but it has many important celebrations which places Jesus in the position to begin his ministry work. The Christmas Season is the second greatest celebration; Easter is the first. Jesus' ministry work begins after he is baptized with water and is filled with the Holy Spirit. The Monday after Jesus' baptism begins Ordinary Time and it is interrupted the Tuesday before Ash Wednesday.

The Christmas Season is a time of jubilation for Christ, our Savior, is born! He is the light of the world showing us the path to the Kingdom of God. He taught us many things like the Lord's Prayer, the Beatitudes, and the Great Commandment: "You shall love the Lord your God with all your heart, with all your soul, with all your mind, and with all your strength." Mark 12:30. Jesus is our saving Lord.

"I AM THE LIGHT OF THE WORLD. WHOEVER FOLLOWS ME WILL NOT WALK IN DARKNESS, BUT WILL HAVE THE LIGHT OF LIFE." JOHN 8:12

Cozy Pork Kabobs

2 -2.5	Pounds of pork loin cubed, salt and pepper to taste
2	Eggs lightly beaten with some water
1	Package of 30 wooden bamboo skewers
1	Package from box of saltines finely crushed

Skewer cubed pork on the bamboo skewers (3 to 4 pieces depending on size of cube). Dip skewered pork in egg, coat with finely crushed saltines, quick brown kabobs in oil and place in a medium to large roaster. Bake at 350° F for 1 to 1½ hours or until pork is done. Yield: about 10 to 15 kabobs depending on size of cubes.

"AND SO THEY LEFT, AND ON THEIR WAY THEY SAW THE SAME STAR THEY HAD SEEN IN THE EAST. WHEN THEY SAW IT, HOW HAPPY THEY WERE, WHAT JOY WAS THEIRS!" MATTHEW 2:9

Pretzel Jell-o

First layer: 2 cups crushed pretzels; 3/4 cup melted butter; 3 tablespoons sugar. Mix together and pat in 13 x 10-inch pan. Bake 8 to 10 minutes at 400° F. Cool completely.

Second layer: 1 8-ounce cream cheese – softened; 1 cup sugar;1 8-ounce cool whip. Blend together and spread on cooled crust.

Third layer: 1 6-ounce strawberry jello;2 cups boiling water; 2 10-ounce packages frozen sliced strawberries. Dissolve jello in boiling water. Stir in frozen berries. When partially set, pour over second layer and refrigerate for four hours or overnight.

"Shout with joy to the Lord,
all the earth; break into song;
sing praise.
Sing praise to the Lord with the harp,
with the harp and melodious song."
Psalms 98:4-5

GALUMPKIS – CABBAGE ROLLS

1 Medium size head of cabbage; 1 Pound of lean ground beef; 1 Cup instant rice partially cooked; ¼ Cup finely chopped onions; 2 Cans condensed tomato soup (10 ¾ ounce each); Salt and pepper to taste

A simple, yet tried and true recipe from the Polish immigrants to America, Galumpkis is a delightful change. Peel off old leaves from cabbage. Cut deep around the core of the cabbage (easier to peel off). Place cabbage head in constant warm water (on the stove) to soften the leaves and partially cook them. Peel the leaves off the core as they become soft. Prepare meat by mixing the partially cooked rice, onions, salt and pepper. Using a large serving spoon, spoon meat mixture onto one leaf, roll once, fold sides in and continue rolling. Place cabbage roll seam down in a roaster. Spoon two cans of condensed tomato soup over rolls, and add ¾ soup can of water at bottom. Cover the rolls with extra cabbage leaves to prevent the rolls from burning. Place roaster cover on and bake at 350° F for 1 ½ hours or until cabbage is tender. The tomato soup at bottom makes for gravy to put on mashed potatoes.

GIVE TO THE LORD, YOU HEAVENLY BEINGS, GIVE TO THE LORD GLORY AND MIGHT; GIVE TO THE LORD THE GLORY DUE GOD'S NAME. BOW DOWN BEFORE THE LORD'S HOLY SPLENDOR! PSALMS 29:1-2

CHEESY POTATOES

1 Package of diced frozen potatoes (2 pound bag thawed)
1 Container of sour cream (8 ounce)
1 Small onion - diced
1 Can of cream of mushroom soup (may need a second can for more moisture)
1 Package of shredded sharp cheddar cheese (8 ounce)
Salt and pepper to taste

Mix all ingredients and place in a crock pot. Cook for 8 hours on low or 4 hours on high.

AND SUDDENLY THERE WAS A MULTITUDE OF HEAVENLY HOST WITH THE ANGEL, PRAISING GOD AND SAYING: "GLORY TO GOD IN THE HIGHEST AND ON EARTH PEACE TO THOSE ON WHOM HIS FAVOR RESTS." LUKE 2:13-14

SIMMERING POTPOURRI

The peels of two oranges and 2 tangerines; 1 whole cinnamon stick; 3 to 4 whole cardamom seeds; 2 to 3 drops of vanilla extract.

Put all ingredients in a medium size saucepan and cover with water at least five inches deep; put on a low heat on the back burner of stove; continually add water as it evaporates; NEVER leave unattended as this may be dangerous!

MANY ARE THE PLANS IN A MAN'S HEART, BUT IT IS THE DECISION OF THE LORD THAT ENDURES.
PROVERB 19:21

A Child is Born

Rejoice and behold a child is born! Give thanks and praise for Jesus our Savior, for he was born into this world for the sake of mankind. O Lord God, we raise our voices rejoicing of the birth of your son. We pray that you will look upon us with loving eyes as you looked upon your son. We pray for our families and friends so they may feel the joy of your son's birth and know the goodness that he will bring to us all. We pray that your son's light will shine within us from this day forth, so we may light the path for others to follow in your son's foot steps. Amen.

Lent

COME WALK WITH ME

Six Sundays and 40 weekdays prepares us for the high feast of Easter. Lent begins on Ash Wednesday and ends on Holy Thursday. In the past, Lent was considered a retreat-like final preparation period for catechumens, those who are entering into the church for the first time (initiated into the church) and into the Paschal mystery at the Easter Vigil. For those who were already apart of the church, Lent is the time of renewal and penance.

The word Lent is from the Anglo-Saxon lencten (spring). The Saxon name for March is lenctentid (springtide) which is the month when the days begin to lengthen (also a root of "lent"). Most of the fasting falls within the month of March. "Then Jesus was led by the Spirit into the desert to be tempted by the devil. He fasted for forty days and forty nights." Matthew 4:1-2

The fourth and fifth Sundays of Lent have significance. For instance, the fourth Sunday of Lent is referred to as the Laetare Sunday, Mothering Sunday, Reflection, and Rose Sunday. "Rejoice with Jerusalem," Isaiah 66:10. The fourth Sunday is a half way point in the penitential season and is marked by the rose vestments worn by the priests instead of violet. The fourth Sunday is joyous because of "handing over" the Apostles' Creed to catechumens. This Sunday is also remembered as children coming home to visit with their mothers. Roses were brought to church and placed on the altar to be blessed and the children celebrated Mass with their mothers.

Many years ago, the church would cover all crucifixes, statues, and pictures in purple cloth from two Sundays before Easter until Good Friday. In those days, the fifth Sunday of Lent, one week before Palm Sunday, was called Passion Sunday or Judica Sunday, after the first word of the introit "Judge me, O Lord…" (from Psalm 43). The veiling expresses sorrow of the church at this time. The unveiling took place on Good Friday.

Holy Week begins with Palm (Passion) Sunday and ended with "Holy Saturday." Palm Sunday was also referred to "Fig Sunday" because figs were eaten that day as a symbol of the fig tree that was cursed by Christ after he entered Jerusalem. When he reached it he found nothing but leaves; it was not the time for figs. And he said to it in reply, "May no one ever eat of your fruit again!" Mark 11:13-14. Mandatum novum da nobis ("I give you a new commandment…" John 13:34) began Holy Thursday also known as Maundy Thursday. The washing of the feet ceremony became a tradition on Holy Thursday. Shear Thursday came about because of an ancient practice of trimming hair and beard that day as a sign of spiritual preparation for Easter.

Today we know Holy Thursday as being the Last Supper. This is the day when Jesus and the twelve apostles met in a special room to celebrate the Passover. Jesus spoke to the apostles about betrayal, crucifixion, and rising on the third day. Jesus taught the apostles about the Bread and Wine – the body and blood of Christ – the Eucharist. During Mass we hear, "happy are they who are called to this supper." Three Hours or Tre Ore refers to Christ's three hours on the cross and the noon-to-three o'clock Good Friday service. The Mass of the Pre-Sanctified, which is not a Mass at all but an old name for the Good Friday service which includes Communion "pre-sanctified" (consecrated the night before). Good Friday today remains the only day of the year without a celebration of the Eucharist. The Eucharist - Jesus - has died.

The Great Service of Light is a part of the Easter Vigil on Holy Saturday. The light of the Paschal candle represents the light Christ brought to us (a darkened world). Tenebrae means "darkness" in Latin. During the evenings of Holy Thursday, Good Friday, and Holy Saturday, the Liturgy had a tone of mourning and a ceremony of light. A triangular stand with fifteen candles was used. One by one the candles would be extinguished and just before the last candle was put out; a prayer was offered in darkness. One candle was relit, and the assembly dispersed in silence.

"FATHER, IF YOU ARE WILLING, TAKE THIS CUP AWAY FROM ME; STILL, NOT MY WILL BUT YOURS BE DONE." LUKE 22:42

FORTY DAY TRAIL MIX

½   Cup of raisins
1   Cup of almonds
1   Pound bag of mini pretzels
1   Cup lightly salted peanuts or cashews
1/3   Cup coarse coconut
1   Box of chocolate chip Teddy Grahams (optional)
1 ½   Cups of mini chocolate chips (omit candy if it has been sacrificed for Lent)

Mix all ingredients in a medium to large bowl. Place into 40 snack bags. Take one snack bag for each day of Lent while meditating.

BUT WHEN YOU FAST, ANOINT YOUR HEAD AND WASH YOUR FACE, SO THAT YOU MAY NOT APPEAR TO BE FASTING, EXCEPT TO YOUR FATHER WHO IS HIDDEN. AND YOUR FATHER WHO SEES WHAT IS HIDDEN WILL REPAY YOU.
MATTHEW 6:17-18

Baked Orange Roughy

1 pound orange roughy fish
1/3 cup finely grated parmesan cheese
¾ cup fine plain bread crumbs
2 tablespoons of butter
3 tablespoons of lemon juice
Salt and pepper to taste

Cut fish into 5 or 6 pieces, rinse. Mix parmesan cheese and bread crumbs and set aside. Mix butter and lemon juice and brush on one side of fish fillets. Place in a shallow baking dish and sprinkle the bread crumb mixture on top of fish. Bake in preheated oven at 350° F for 30 minutes or until fish flakes apart with a fork.

Orange Roughy is a tender white fish with a mild flavor.

JESUS CRIED OUT AND SAID, "WHOEVER BELIEVES IN ME BELIEVES NOT ONLY IN ME BUT ALSO IN THE ONE WHO SENT ME, AND WHOEVER SEES ME SEES THE ONE WHO SENT ME." JOHN 12:44

APPLE BREAD

2 Eggs; 1 cup sugar; ¼ cup butter; 1 teaspoon soda; 2 tablespoon buttermilk (or sour milk*); 2 cups sifted flour;   ½ teaspoon salt; 2 cups diced raw apples; ½ cup chopped nuts (optional)

*Regular milk with a little vinegar added may be substituted. Cream together the eggs, butter, and sugar. Mix soda with sour milk (or buttermilk). Add dry ingredients. Mix well. Stir in apples and nuts. Place in bread pan, lightly greased and floured.

Topping: 2 tablespoons flour; 2 tablespoons sugar; 1 teaspoon cinnamon; 2 tablespoon butter, melted.

Mix topping ingredients together. Sprinkle topping on dough and bake at 350° for 1 hour.

"THIS IS THE TIME OF FULFILLMENT. THE KINGDOM OF GOD IS AT HAND. REPENT, AND BELIEVE IN THE GOSPEL."
MARK 1:15

Quick Cinnamon Rolls

2 Loaves of frozen bread; 1 Stick of butter; 1 cup brown sugar
1/3 Cup sugar; 1 Teaspoon cinnamon; 3 Tablespoons of milk

Glaze: 4 tablespoons melted margarine; 1 cup powdered sugar; 1 table spoon of milk

Thaw bread dough in a refrigerator overnight. In the morning grease a 9x13 inch baking dish. Break one loaf of the thawed bread into walnut size pieces and distribute them on the bottom of the pan; pieces should touch. Melt together the margarine, brown sugar, white sugar, cinnamon and milk and drizzle over the dough pieces. Break the second loaf into walnut size pieces and put over the first layer. Let this rise until double in size (about 2 hours). Bake in a preheated oven at 375 degrees for 25 minutes. While still warm, drizzle with the glaze. Glaze: beat together melted margarine, powdered sugar and milk.

BUT TO THE PENITENT HE PROVIDES A WAY BACK, HE ENCOURAGES THOSE WHO ARE LOSING HOPE! RETURN TO THE LORD AND GIVE UP SIN, PRAY TO HIM AND MAKE YOUR OFFENSES FEW. SIRACH 17:19-20

Rueben Casserole

1 Package of egg noodles
1 Package smoked sausage, cut into bite size pieces
1 or 2 Cans of Cream of Mushroom soup (this depends on the size package of noodles)
1 Can of sauerkraut (16 ounce) drained
Enough Swiss cheese slices to cover dish

Cook noodles according to package directions, place in greased baking dish. Mix sausage, soup, sauerkraut with noodles. Bake for about 40 minutes in a 350 degree oven. Place Swiss cheese slices over casserole and bake until melted.

"Amen, I say to you, this poor widow put in more than all the other contributors to the treasury. For they have all contributed from their surplus wealth, but she, from her poverty, has contributed all she had, her whole livelihood."
Mark 12:43-44

PREPARE OUR HEARTS

In the solitude of my room, I pray to you Lord for guidance in being more like your son Jesus who willing sacrificed his life for us. I pray that my sins are forgiven and I feel joy within my heart. These forty days before the great feast of Easter, I ask that you hear my prayers, hear my cries, and take away my sorrows. In the solitude of my room, I pray to you O Lord my God. Amen

Easter Season

SING ALLELUIA - CHRIST THE LORD IS RISEN TODAY

The Great Fifty Days from Easter Sunday to Pentecost Sunday is the time we celebrate Christ's victory over death and saving grace for us. Easter coming from the Norse term Eostur, the season of the rising sun, or the time of the new birth of spring. Both these symbolisms gave the Christians symbolism of new life of the risen Christ, the eternal light. "Why do you seek the living one among the dead? He is not here, but he has been raised." Luke 24:5-6

From Easter Sunday to the next Sunday the church refers these days as the "Bright Week" an eight-day week with Easter being the high feast and the following Sunday the low feast. Those who were baptized during the year were encouraged to wear white on Easter Sunday signifying being 'clothed' in Christ and to celebrate this by wearing new clothes.

Between Easter Sunday and Ascension Thursday, Jesus appeared to the apostles and others on several occasions. Mary Magdalene and the holy women were the first to see Jesus since he was raised. When they had seen Jesus, they ran to the others and told them what they saw. Peter was the first of the twelve apostles that Jesus revealed of himself. He was considered to be called to strengthen the faith of his brothers. When Jesus appeared to the apostles he would say, "Peace be with you." Luke 24:36

At one time the Christ candle was extinguished on Ascension Thursday, representing the physical departure of Christ from earth. Now, the Christ candle remains lit though Pentecost, the entire Easter Season. The days between Ascension Thursday and Pentecost Sunday are considered days of anticipation of the coming of the Holy Spirit. The apostles prayed with expectant faith for the Paraclete (comforter, Holy Spirit). There are nine days between Christ's ascension and the Spirit's decent.

Pentecost (Whitsunday) is on the fiftieth day of Easter. It is the day the Holy Spirit descends upon the apostles with "tongues of fire." "Then there appeared to them tongues as of fire, which parted and came to rest on each one of them. And they were all filled with the holy Spirit..." Acts 2:3-4. Pentecost Sunday ends the Easter Season.

The Easter Season is truly a time to celebrate because Christ's resurrection has significance to our faith. The resurrection of Christ fulfilled the promises of the Old Testament and that of what Jesus told while living his earthly life. John 8:28 states, "When you have lifted up the Son of man, then you will know that I am he," confirms the truth of Jesus' divinity. The Paschal mystery tells us: by his death, Christ liberates us from sin; by his Resurrection, he opens for us the way to a new life.

Romans 6:4 states, "so that as Christ was raised from the dead by the glory of the Father, we too might walk in newness of life." This is referring to the new life given to us by Christ's resurrection which reinstates us in God's grace. Furthermore, Christ's resurrection, that is, the risen Christ himself, is the principle and source of our future resurrection.

"CHRIST HAS BEEN RAISED FROM THE DEAD, THE FIRST FRUITS OF THOSE WHO HAVE FALLEN ASLEEP...FOR AS IN ADAM ALL DIE, SO ALSO IN CHRIST SHALL ALL BE MADE ALIVE."
1 CORINTHIANS 15:20-22.

Fruit Bowl Medley

1	Pint of fresh blueberries
2	Red Delicious apples cut into thin slices
1	Quart of fresh strawberries cut into pieces
1	Pint of fresh raspberries
1	Cup of red seedless grapes cut into halves
2	Pears cut into bite size pieces
2	Bananas sliced thin
½	Cup chopped walnuts (optional)
1	8-ounce vanilla flavored yogurt

Mix all ingredients in a medium to large bowl. Chill at least one hour before serving.

FOR IN ONE SPIRIT WE WERE ALL BAPTIZED INTO ONE BODY, WHETHER JEWS OR GREEKS, SLAVES OR FREE PERSONS, AND WE WERE ALL GIVEN TO DRINK OF ONE SPIRIT. 1 CORINTHIANS 12:13

MARY'S EASTER BARS

2 Cups packed brown sugar; 1 Cup butter; 2 Eggs; 2 Cups flour; 1 teaspoon baking powder; ¼ Teaspoon baking soda; 1 Cup M & M chocolate candy pieces – Easter colors; 2 Teaspoon vanilla; 1 Teaspoon almond extract; 1 Cup chopped nuts (optional)

Pre-heat oven to 350 degrees. Grease a 13 x 9 x 2-inch baking pan. In medium saucepan heat brown sugar and butter until smooth, stirring constantly. Cool slightly. Stir in eggs, one at a time. Stir in vanilla and almond extract. Stir in flour. Spread batter in pan. Sprinkle with M & M chocolate candy pieces and nuts. Bake for 25 to 30 minutes or until toothpick comes out clean. Cool slightly, cut when warm.

THUS IT IS WRITTEN THAT THE MESSIAH WOULD SUFFER AND RISE FROM THE DEAD ON THE THIRD DAY AND THAT REPENTANCE, FOR THE FORGIVENESS OF SINS, WOULD BE PREACHED IN HIS NAME TO ALL THE NATIONS, BEGINNING FROM JERUSALEM.
JOHN 24:46

FRENCH TOAST CASSEROLE

5	Cups bread cubes
4	Eggs
1 ½	Cups milk
¼	Cup white sugar, divided
¼	Teaspoon salt
1	Tablespoon margarine, softened
1	Teaspoon ground cinnamon
1	Teaspoon vanilla extract

Preheat oven to 350 degrees F (175 degrees C). Lightly butter an 8x8 inch baking pan. Line bottom of pan with bread cubes. In a large bowl, beat together eggs, milk, 2 tablespoons sugar, salt and vanilla. Pour egg mixture over bread. Dot with margarine; let stand for 10 minutes. Combine remaining 2 tablespoons sugar with 1 teaspoon cinnamon and sprinkle over the top. Bake in preheated oven about 45 to 50 minutes, until top is golden.

"I HAVE EAGERLY DESIRED TO EAT THIS PASSOVER WITH YOU BEFORE I SUFFER, FOR, I TELL YOU, I SHALL NOT EAT IT [AGAIN] UNTIL THERE IS FULFILLMENT IN THE KINGDOM OF GOD."
LUKE 22:15

Cinnamon Treat Breakaways

1	Tube of dinner rolls (package of 10)
¼	Cup melted butter (may need more)
1	Cup of white sugar
1	Tablespoon of cinnamon

Mix sugar and cinnamon together and set aside. Remove dinner rolls from package and separate. Cut each roll in half. Roll each half into a ball. Dip ball into melted butter and coat with sugar mixture. Place coated ball in center of a pizza pan or 8-9 inch cake pan. Continue rolling, dipping, and coating. Place each ball around the first until all the dinner rolls are used up. Preheat oven at 400° F. Place pan in the center of the oven rack. Bake for 10 minutes or until golden brown. If using a pizza pan, remove treats with spatulas and place on a plate.

THEN HE TOOK THE BREAD, SAID THE BLESSING, BROKE IT, AND GAVE IT TO THEM, SAYING, "THIS IS MY BODY, WHICH WILL BE GIVEN FOR YOU; DO THIS IN MEMORY OF ME."
LUKE 22:19

SUNDAY BRUNCH CASSEROLE

½ Pound bacon
½ Cup of onion, chopped
½ Cup green pepper, chopped
12 Eggs
1 Cup of milk
1 Package of frozen hash brown potatoes, thawed (16 ounce)
1 Cup cheddar cheese, shredded
¼ Teaspoon ground mustard
Salt and pepper to taste

Cook bacon until crisp, crumble. Sauté onions and green pepper until tender. Beat eggs and milk in a large bowl. Stir in onion, green pepper and the remaining ingredients. Pour into a greased 13x9 inch baking pan and bake at 350 degrees for 35 to 45 minutes. To check for doneness, insert a knife into the center; when it comes out clean, the dish is done.

BLESSED BE THE GOD AND FATHER OF OUR LORD JESUS CHRIST, WHO IN HIS GREAT MERCY GAVE US A NEW BIRTH TO A LIVING HOPE THROUGH THE RESURRECTION OF JESUS CHRIST FROM THE DEAD. 1 PETER 1:3

Rejoice, the Lord is Risen

O God of mercy hear our songs of praise, for your son has risen today. We sing with gladden hearts for your grace is upon us. The path to your Kingdom is lit by the resurrection of Jesus. We pray that the path stays clear and we do not stumble as we walk our faith journey. We ask that you keep the Holy Spirit with us to guide us, to give us wisdom, and flood us with knowledge. We pray that your grace continues to rain upon us so we may enter into your Kingdom. Alleluia the Lord is Risen! Amen.

ORDINARY TIME...A TIME TO REFLECT

Ordinary Time is from the Monday after Pentecost Sunday to the end of the Church year (the beginning of Advent). During Ordinary Time there are some notable Sundays: Trinity Sunday, Body and Blood of Christ, Christ the King, and Nativity of John the Baptist. Ordinary Time also gives us the opportunity to "catch" our breath from the joyous celebrations of Christmas and Easter.

With Ordinary Time being a more quiet time of the church year, this may be a good place to mention the Mass. Mass begins with the introductory Rites and ends with the concluding Rite. In between are the two great parts of the Mass, the Liturgy of the Word and the Liturgy of the Eucharist.

The Introductory Rite includes a greeting and an expression of our sorrow for our sins by reciting the Penitential prayer or Penitential Rite. "I confess to almighty God and to you, my brothers and sisters, that I have sinned through my own fault..." We then ask for Jesus' mercy.

"Glory to God in the highest, and peace to his people on earth...." Praising God comes before the Liturgy of the Word. As we sit, we listen to the First and Second Readings. During most of the church year, the First Reading comes from the Old Testament - God speaking to us through the Prophets. The Second Readings come from the New Testament - God speaking to us through the Apostles. The Gospel from the New Testament is God speaking to us through Jesus – the Word.

The altar is prepared for the Liturgy of the Eucharist by presenting the Gifts - bread and wine to the priest. In the Liturgy of the Eucharist, the priest offers up the bread, "Blessed are you, Lord, God of all creation. Through your goodness we have this bread to offer..." Then the wine is offered up. More prayers are said and the people respond in kind. Through the Eucharistic prayer we give thanks and praise to God. More prayers are offered. Then the bread and wine is consecrated much as it was done at the Last Supper.

The Great Amen, the Lord's Prayer, sign of peace, and the breaking of the bread take place before we may process to the altar to receive the Body and Blood of Christ. We also kneel with bowed heads and say, "... Lord, I am not worthy to receive you, but only say the word and I shall be healed."

The Mass is a wonderful way to celebrate the Eucharist, Jesus, the Bread of Life. One special Mass celebrated during Ordinary Time is the Trinity Sunday which is the Sunday after Pentecost. Trinity Sunday unites the church as one; through one God we have the Father, the Son, and the Holy Spirit - a Divine Trinity. John the Baptist said, "...'On whomever you see the Spirit come down and remain, he is the one who will baptize with the holy Spirit.' Now I have seen and testified that he is the Son of God." John 1:33-34. Baptizing Jesus was an important task for John the Baptist because it fulfilled a prophecy from the Old Testament.

June 24th is the feast day of John the Baptist. We honor him because of his role in fulfilling prophecies of the Old Testament. He was the instrument of God's will to provide for us a means in which to renew our faith through the sacrament of baptism.

THEY DEVOTED THEMSELVES TO THE TEACHING OF THE APOSTLES AND TO THE COMMUNAL LIFE, TO THE BREAKING OF THE BREAD AND TO THE PRAYERS.
ACTS 3:42

Summertime Punch

32 fluid ounces Hawaiian Fruit Punch
12 ounce lemonade concentrate
12 ounce orange juice concentrate
12 ounce pineapple juice concentrate
1 liter (about 16 fluid ounces) bottle of ginger ale
32 ounces of water by using one juice container above

Mix all the juices and lemonade and half of the ginger ale. Add ice cubes to chill.

"Turn away from your sins and be baptized, and God will forgive your sins." Luke 3:3

BLUEBERRY COBBLER

1 stick butter
2 cups self-rising flour
2 cups sugar
2 cups milk
6-7 cups fresh blueberries

Preheat oven to 350° F. Melt butter in 13x9x2 inch baking dish in oven. This only takes a few seconds. Remove the baking dish from the oven and place on a heat resistant surface as you finish.

In a mixing bowl, stir the flour and sugar together, add milk and blend until smooth. Pour on top of melted butter. Pour fruit over top. Do not stir into batter. Bake 45 to 60 minutes.

For fresh berries: add ¾ cups of sugar to 6-7 cups of berries. Cook 5-6 minutes on medium heat while preparing the above.

"THE EARTH IS THE LORD'S AND ALL IT HOLDS, THE WORLD AND THOSE WHO LIVE THERE. FOR GOD FOUNDED IT ON THE SEAS, ESTABLISHED IT OVER THE RIVERS."
PSALM 24:1-2

Zesty Spaghetti and Vegetable Medley

1   Pound of thin spaghetti noodles; cooked and cooled; 1 Tomato diced about 1 inch in size; 1 Green bell pepper - 1 x ¼ inch slices; 1 Medium cucumber cubed; ½ cup red onion coarsely chopped; 1 Cup small broccoli florets; 1 Cup small cauliflower florets; ½ Cup finely chopped celery; ¾ Cup chopped carrots; 1 Small can of black olives drained - optional; 1 Bottle of Zesty Italian dressing

Ham cubes or shredded ham or quartered pepperoni may be added to the recipe. Mix the vegetables and meat with the cooked noodles. Use just enough dressing to coat everything and refrigerate for at least 1 hour or overnight. Just before serving, add more dressing to moisten the salad mixture. Top with pine nuts for different taste. Pine nuts are located in the baking section.

FINALLY, ALL OF YOU, BE OF ONE MIND, SYMPATHETIC, LOVING TOWARD ONE ANOTHER, COMPASSIONATE, HUMBLE. DO NOT RETURN EVIL FOR EVIL, OR INSULT FOR INSULT; BUT, ON THE CONTRARY, A BLESSING, BECAUSE TO THIS YOU WERE CALLED, THAT YOU MIGHT INHERIT A BLESSING.
1 PETER 3:8

SPINACH SALAD

2 Cups fresh baby spinach leaves; pre-washed works well
½ Cup raw pea pods
½ cup sliced fresh strawberries
¼ Cup thin red onion slices
2 Tablespoons sliced almond, toasted
¼ Cup Catalina Dressing; any brand; light or regular

To toast almonds: put almonds in a heavy non-stick skillet on medium high heat for 3-4 minutes or until golden brown. Toss all ingredients in a large bowl and serve.

A GOOD NAME IS MORE DESIRABLE THAN GREAT RICHES, AND HIGH ESTEEM, THAN GOLD AND SILVER. RICH AND POOR HAVE A COMMON BOND:
THE LORD IS THE MAKER OF THEM ALL.
PROVERBS 22:1-2

Taco Salad

1 Head of lettuce washed and cut into pieces
1 Pound of lean ground beef
1 Package of taco seasoning
2 Green onions diced with some of the greens
1 Package 12 ounce shredded cheddar cheese or taco mix cheese
2 Tomatoes diced
1 Cup coarse pieces of tortilla or Dorito chips
French Catalina or Thousand Island dressing

Brown the meat with the taco seasoning – drain the fat. In a large bowl mix all vegetables, meat, cheese and enough dressing to coat everything. Leave the tortilla chips for just before serving. Add the tortilla or favorite flavored chips, lightly toss to coat and serve.

BELOVED, LET US LOVE ONE ANOTHER, BECAUSE LOVE IS OF GOD; EVERYONE WHO LOVES IS BEGOTTEN BY GOD AND KNOWS GOD.
1 JOHN 4:7

A TIME TO REST

Summer followed by autumn is a time for rest; a time to reflect upon the church's great seasons of Easter and Christmas. Heavenly Father we pray that the joyous feeling we experienced during Easter and Christmas does not diminish during the summer and autumn seasons. We pray that our faith was strengthen from the celebrations of Easter and Christmas. We ask that the Holy Spirit stays with us during these restful months so we will not lose the knowledge gained. We pray for guidance when we begin to waiver and we pray for your grace when we have pleased you. Although this is a time for rest, we ask that you always be there for us. Amen.

MAY THE PEACE OF THE LORD BE WITH YOU

The church year flows from one marvelous season to another. We have the dawning of Advent which gives us the opportunity to prepare ourselves for the birth of Christ. The Christmas Season follows Advent and walks us through to Epiphany Sunday. Jesus, the Light of World begins to shine brighter for us so we may follow him.

Ordinary Time follows the Christmas Season but is interrupted the Tuesday before Ash Wednesday. Ash Wednesday is the start of Lent a time for praying, fasting and readying ourselves for the Greatest Season of the church – Easter.

Easter is the time when Christ fulfills what the prophets from the Old Testament has told. Then he said: "Listen, O house of David! Is it not enough for you to weary men, must you also weary my God? Therefore the Lord himself will give you this sign: the virgin shall be with child, and bear a son, and shall name him Immanuel." Isaiah 7:13-14.

Pentecost Sunday concludes the Easter Season and Ordinary Time resumes. Ordinary Time takes us through the summer and fall months. It is a time to relax and catch our breaths before the church season begins again. The following resources were used to obtain the faith information in this book and they are a good source to learn more about the Catholic faith.

Catechism of the Catholic Church. USA copyright © 1994, United States Catholic Conference, Inc. – Libreria Editrice Vaticana.

My Picture Missal. Copyright © 1978 by Catholic Book Publishing Co. New York.

The Catholic Bible. New American Bible, Personal Study Edition. Copyright © 1995 by Oxford University Press, Inc.

The Catholic Encyclopedia. New Advent www.NewAdvent.org. Copyright 1907-1922 by Robert Appleton Company and The Encyclopedia Press, Inc. Computer edition copyright 2003 by Kevin Knight.

The Catholic Source Book. Third Edition. Copyright © 2000 by Harcourt Religion Publishers.

Good News Bible. Today's English Version – Second Edition copyright 1992 The American Bible Society.

Printed in the United States
84358LV00002B